TEX MEX

KÖNEMANN

Talking Tex-Mex

The phrase 'Tex-Mex' isn't a trendy term coined by some food writer, or a funny name for a Mexican restaurant—it is a geographical fact. The border between Mexico and Texas may separate two very different countries, but where food is concerned, the line blurs.

Tex-Mex food relies heavily on traditional Mexican, and therefore often Spanish, ingredients and recipes, but there is also a strong American influence. While the origins are ancient, it is very modern food, quick and easy to prepare and, if you go easy on the cheese and sour cream, quite healthy. It is also great for vegetarians, with plenty of bean dishes. We are all familiar with Tex-Mex dishes such as tacos, nachos and chilli con carne, whereas dishes such as tamales and chicken mole are less familiar, as are some of the ingredients. A glossary over the page explains the less well-known ingredients, while on this page are definitions of some Tex-Mex dishes (with the pronunciations where necessary), which will have you speaking fluent Tex-Mex in no time at all.

Burrito
(*ber-ee-toh*) Meaning literally 'little donkey', a burrito is a flour tortilla rolled around a savoury filling of shredded beef, chicken or refried beans.

Chilli Con Carne
A subject close to the heart of any Texan is chilli. There are as many recipes for chilli as there are cooks in Texas, each one touted as the best, the most authentic and the most traditional. Ironically, probably the least authentic version is the one most people are familiar with, based on minced beef, with tomatoes and kidney beans. A true Texan would deride it as a glorified Bolognese sauce, but of course we have included it in this book—for the gringos!

Chilli Con Queso
(*chih-lee kon kay-soh*) Literally 'chilli with cheese' (or cheese with chillies!)

Chimichanga
(chee-mee-chan-gah)
A flour tortilla filled usually with meat or chicken, folded envelope style and fried in oil until crisp.

Enchilada
(en-chuh-lah-da)
A corn tortilla filled with beans, beef or chicken, rolled, topped with tomato sauce and then baked.

Fajitas
(fah-hee-tuhs) Originally referring to the cut of meat (skirt steak), now understood as marinated beef, chicken or seafood, cooked on a sizzling cast-iron plate and served with salsa, cheese, guacamole and lettuce, with flour tortillas for wrapping.

Guacamole
Mashed avocado, often flavoured with onion, coriander, tomato and lime juice. Great as a dip or to accompany other Tex-Mex dishes.

Huevos Rancheros
(way-vohs rahn-cheh-ros) Huevos are eggs, rancheros means ranch-style. The eggs are poached or fried and served on crisp fried corn tortillas, with a tomato 'ranch' sauce. A great breakfast for curing a hangover!

Quesadilla
(keh-sah-dee-yah)
In Mexico, this is a turnover made from a corn pastry, filled and deep-fried. A Tex-Mex quesadilla, however, is two flour tortillas sandwiched together with cheese and beef, chicken, beans (or any leftovers that seem suitable!), and pan-fried. The simplest quesadilla, filled with cheese and chillies, is really a Tex-Mex grilled cheese sandwich.

Refried beans
This sounds like the beans have been fried twice, but it actually translates as 'well-fried' beans, meaning that after being boiled until tender, they are then fried until very soft.

Salsa Literally meaning just a 'sauce', salsa is, however, usually used to describe an uncooked condiment, such as tomato, onion and coriander.

Tamales A dough is made from masa harina (see glossary), then wrapped in corn husks with a chicken or meat mixture, and steamed.

Tostadas A corn tortilla, fried to crisp, and topped with layers of beans, beef or chicken, cheese and salad.

3

ANCHO

BLACK BEANS

JALAPEÑOS

MASA HARINA

MULATO

Tex-Mex Glossary

If you can't get hold of some of the special chillies shown here, just use the more common long chillies or small bird's eye chillies instead.

Ancho
This deep-red dried poblano chilli is the most common Mexican dried chilli variety. It has a sweet, fruity flavour and a mild heat. The Ancho, along with the mulato and pasilla chillies, is considered one of the 'holy trinity' of chillies. Combined together, these 3 chillies are the essential ingredient in Mexican moles.

Black beans
Native to Yucatan, Mexico, these beans have purpley-black skins, creamy white flesh and a slightly smoky flavour. Black beans are also known as turtle beans and are available dried or canned. Do not confuse these beans with Asian fermented black beans.

Chilli powder
Dried red chillies are finely ground to make this powder. The powders are marked 'hot' or 'mild', but the heat will differ between manufacturers. A Mexican chilli powder is also often available.

Choko
Known as chayote in the USA, this pale, green, pear-shaped fruit is related to the gourd and was a staple food of the Aztecs and Mayas. It has a crisp texture and a subtle flavour suitable for casseroles and salsas.

Coriander
Also known as cilantro, coriander is an essential ingredient in salsas and sauces. The leaves have a fresh, pungent, peppery flavour and a bright green colour, which complement spicy foods very well.

Cornmeal
Cornmeal is produced by grinding dried corn kernels. It is used as a thickener, filling or to coat. Available finely or coarsely ground, cornmeal is often labelled as polenta.

Habanero
Said to be the hottest of the fresh chillies, the habanero changes from green to orange to red, and can be used at any of these stages. It is one for the chilli fanatic.

Jalapeño
This popular fresh chilli is smooth and thick-fleshed and available in red or green. The skin sometimes has fine brown cracks running along it. Canned jalapeños are also often available.

Masa harina
Dried corn kernels are soaked, then finely ground to produce this flour, which can be white or blue and is used to prepare tamales, corn tortillas and corn chips.

Mulato
This dark brown chilli is a variety of dried poblano. It has dried-fruit and chocolate flavours with moderate heat. It is one of the 'holy trinity' of chillies.

Pasilla
Also known as chile negro due to its blackish colour, this dried chilli is a member of the 'holy trinity' of chillies. Its deep, intense flavour ranges from raisin and berry to coffee and smoke.

Pepitas
Pepitas are green pumpkin seeds, which can be eaten lightly toasted as a snack or used to thicken and flavour moles and other sauces.

Pinto beans
A variety of red kidney beans, pintos have streaky reddish-brown skin, which becomes pink when cooked. Pintos can be replaced with red kidney beans if they are unavailable.

Poblano
This is a large, mild to hot chilli with a thick flesh and subtle smoky flavour. It is usually roasted and stuffed, rather than chopped and added to dishes. When dried, it is called an Ancho chilli.

Red kidney beans
Widely available in both dried and canned forms, these full-flavoured beans have a dark red skin and creamy coloured flesh.

Serrano
Available in red and green, this fresh chilli is commonly used after it has matured to red. Smooth and moderately hot, it is often used in salsas and sauces.

Tomatillo
The shape and flavour of this green fruit resembles a small unripe tomato, but it is actually a member of the Cape gooseberry family. Tomatillos are available canned from speciality food stores and fresh in the USA.

PASILLA

PEPITAS

PINTO BEANS

POBLANO

TOMATILLOS

Tex-Mex

Most Tex-Mex dishes are quick and easy to make and taste delicious—great for a quick dinner or instead of fast food.

Beef Fajitas

Preparation time:
  30 minutes
  + overnight standing
Total cooking time:
  15 minutes
Serves 4

1 kg (2 lb) rump steak
3/4 cup (185 ml/6 fl oz)
  olive oil
2 tablespoons lime juice
4 cloves garlic, chopped
3 red chillies, chopped
2 tablespoons tequila
  (optional)
1 red capsicum, thinly
  sliced
1 yellow capsicum,
  thinly sliced
1 red onion, thinly
  sliced
8 flour tortillas (ready-
  made or see page 22)

1. Place the meat in a dish. Pour over the combined oil, lime juice, garlic, chillies and tequila and season with pepper. Cover and marinate overnight, turning once. Drain.

2. Preheat the oven to warm 160°C (315°F/ Gas 2–3). Heat a cast-iron or heavy-based pan. Add the meat in batches and cook over high heat for 4–5 minutes each side. Cool, then slice and toss with the capsicum and onion.

3. Heat some oil in the pan over high heat. Place some of the meat mixture into the pan and toss well for about 2–3 minutes, searing the meat. Meanwhile, wrap the tortillas in foil and place in the oven for 10 minutes to soften. Place the fajitas on a serving plate and serve with the tortillas, shredded lettuce, Guacamole (see page 60), Fresh Corn and Tomato Salsa (see page 39) and sour cream.

NUTRITION PER SERVE
Protein 120 g; Fat 60 g; Carbohydrate 25 g; Dietary Fibre 3 g; Cholesterol 335 mg; 4850 kJ (1160 cal)

Beef Fajitas

Classic Quesadillas

Preparation time:
  15 minutes
Total cooking time:
  10 minutes
Serves 2–4

4 flour tortillas (ready-
  made or see page 22)
2 cups (250 g/8 oz)
  grated Cheddar
6 spring onions, finely
  chopped
4 jalapeño chillies,
  seeded and finely
  sliced

1. Brush 1 side of each tortilla with a little oil. Heat a frying pan, then add a tortilla, oiled-side-down. Sprinkle with half the Cheddar, spring onion and chilli.
2. Put another tortilla on top, oiled-side-up. When the bottom is lightly browned, place a plate over the pan, turn the quesadilla out, then slide it back into the pan, cooked tortilla on top. Cook until the quesadilla is brown and the cheese melted, then remove from the pan and keep warm. Repeat with the rest of the tortillas and filling.
3. Cut into wedges and serve with Fresh Tomato Salsa.

Classic Quesadillas (top), Fresh Tomato Salsa, and Vegetarian Quesadillas (bottom)

NUTRITION PER SERVE (4)
*Protein 20 g; Fat 30 g;
Carbohydrate 20 g; Dietary
Fibre 2 g; Cholesterol
60 mg; 1680 kJ (400 cal)*

Vegetarian Quesadillas

Preparation time:
  *15 minutes + 1 hour
  standing*
Total cooking time:
  2 hours 10 minutes
Serves 2–4

1 cup (220 g/7 oz)
  dried black beans
500 g (1 lb) sweet
  potato, cut into thick
  slices
1 large red onion, cut
  into 8 wedges
1¼ cups (185 g/6 oz)
  feta cheese, crumbled
¾ cup (90 g/3 oz)
  grated Cheddar
4 flour tortillas (ready-
  made or see page 22)

1. Place the beans in a pan, cover with water and bring to the boil. Turn off the heat and leave to stand, covered, for 1 hour. Drain, refill with water, bring to the boil and simmer for 1 hour, or until tender. Drain and cool.
2. Brush the sweet potato and onion lightly with olive oil. Roast in a hot 210°C (415°F/Gas 6–7) oven for 1 hour, turning once, until tender. Cool and chop. Combine the beans and vegetables in a bowl with the feta and Cheddar. Use this filling to prepare the quesadillas as instructed above.

NUTRITION PER SERVE (4)
*Protein 30 g; Fat 25 g;
Carbohydrate 50 g; Dietary
Fibre 10 g; Cholesterol
50 mg; 2160 kJ (515 cal)*

Fresh Tomato Salsa

Preparation time:
  5 minutes
Total cooking time:
  Nil
Serves 2–4

4 ripe tomatoes, finely
  chopped
1 small red onion,
  finely chopped
1 jalapeño chilli or red
  chilli, seeded and
  chopped
¼ cup (15 g/½ oz)
  chopped fresh
  coriander
1 tablespoon lime juice

1. Combine all the ingredients in a bowl and mix well. Cover with plastic wrap and refrigerate until ready to use.

NUTRITION PER SERVE (4)
*Protein 2 g; Fat 0 g;
Carbohydrate 4 g; Dietary
Fibre 2 g; Cholesterol
0 mg; 125 kJ (30 cal)*

Breakfast Burritos

Preparation time:
  20 minutes
Total cooking time:
  45 minutes
Serves 4

800 g (1 lb 10 oz)
  potatoes
60 g (2 oz) butter
1 tablespoon oil
4 flour tortillas (ready-
  made or see page 22)
4 spring onions, finely
  chopped
8 eggs, lightly beaten
1 cup (125 g/4 oz)
  grated Cheddar
1 cup (250 ml/8 fl oz)
  Red Chilli Sauce (see
  page 38)
1 cup (250 ml/8 fl oz)
  Green Chilli Sauce
  (see page 38)

1. Preheat the oven to warm 160°C (315°F/ Gas 2–3). Peel the potatoes and chop into cubes. Cook in a large pan of boiling salted water for about 20 minutes, or until just tender (don't overcook or they will go mushy). Drain well.
2. Heat half the butter and the oil in a heavy-based frying pan, add the potato and cook for about 10 minutes over medium heat, or until golden brown, turning occasionally. Meanwhile, wrap the flour tortillas in foil and place in the oven for 10 minutes to soften.
3. In a separate pan, melt the remaining butter, add the spring onion and cook for 1 minute, then add the eggs and cook until set, stirring occasionally.
4. To serve, place a quarter of the potato and a quarter of the egg mixture into the centre of each tortilla, sprinkle each with a quarter of the Cheddar and roll up. Spoon over the chilli sauces and serve.

NUTRITION PER SERVE
Protein 30 g; Fat 50 g; Carbohydrate 60 g; Dietary Fibre 10 g; Cholesterol 430 mg; 3220 kJ (770 cal)

Huevos Rancheros

Preparation time:
  25 minutes
Total cooking time:
  30 minutes
Serves 4

1 red jalapeño chilli
3 large tomatoes, finely
  chopped
1 small onion, finely
  chopped
1 clove garlic,
  crushed
1 tablespoon chopped
  fresh coriander
3 tablespoons oil
8 corn tortillas (ready-
  made or see page 22)
8 eggs

1. Roast the chilli by holding with tongs in a gas flame, or by flattening out and cooking under a preheated grill, until the skin is black and blistered. Place in a plastic bag to cool, then scrape away the skin. Discard the seeds and finely chop the chilli.
2. To make the tomato sauce, combine the chopped tomato with the onion, garlic, coriander and jalapeño chilli in a small pan. Bring to the boil, then reduce the heat and simmer for 10 minutes, or until the mixture has thickened.
3. Heat the oil in a frying pan and cook the corn tortillas one at a time until warmed through and just crispy. Drain on paper towels and keep warm.
4. Fry the eggs a few at a time in the oil remaining in the pan. To serve, arrange 2 tortillas on each plate. Top with the tomato sauce and 2 eggs. Serve immediately, with a spoonful of Refried Beans (see page 63) on the side.

NUTRITION PER SERVE
Protein 20 g; Fat 25 g; Carbohydrate 40 g; Dietary Fibre 4 g; Cholesterol 360 mg; 1900 kJ (450 cal)

Breakfast Burritos (top) with Huevos Rancheros

Red-Hot Ribs

Preparation time:
 10 minutes
 + marinating
Total cooking time:
 1 hour 20 minutes
Serves 4

*1.5 kg (3 lb) American-
 style pork ribs*
*1 small onion, roughly
 chopped*
2 cloves garlic, chopped
*2 small chillies, seeded
 and finely chopped*
*2 cups (500 ml/16 fl oz)
 tomato sauce*
*1/4 cup (55 g/2 oz)
 firmly packed soft
 brown sugar*
*1 1/2 cups (375 ml/
 12 fl oz) dark beer*

1. Cut the racks of ribs
into pieces, with 3 or
4 ribs in each piece.
2. Put the onion, garlic
and chilli in a food
processor, and process
until finely chopped.
Add the tomato sauce,
sugar and beer and
process until combined.
3. Place the sauce
mixture into a large
pan. Add the ribs and
bring to the boil.
Reduce the heat and
simmer for 1 hour,
partially covered,
moving the ribs
occasionally to ensure
even cooking.

4. Taste the sauce and
add more chilli if
desired. Transfer the
ribs and the marinade
to a shallow, non-
metallic dish, cover and
refrigerate for several
hours or overnight.
5. Drain the ribs,
reserving the marinade,
and place on a greased
preheated barbecue or
grill. Cook for about
15 minutes over high
heat, turning and
brushing occasionally
with the marinade. If
you like, heat the
remaining marinade in
a pan until boiling and
simmer for 5 minutes.
Serve with the ribs.

NUTRITION PER SERVE
*Protein 55 g; Fat 100 g;
Carbohydrate 35 g; Dietary
Fibre 2 g; Cholesterol
375 mg; 5835 kJ (1394 cal)*

Potato Skins with Chilli Con Queso

Preparation time:
 20 minutes
Total cooking time:
 1 hour 20 minutes
Serves 4 as a starter

4 large potatoes
oil, for deep-frying

Chilli Con Queso
30 g (1 oz) butter
*2 spring onions, finely
 sliced*

*1 small red chilli, finely
 chopped*
1 clove garlic, crushed
*3/4 cup (185 g/6 oz)
 sour cream*
*2 cups (250 g/8 oz)
 grated Cheddar*

1. Preheat the oven to
hot 210°C (415°F/Gas
6–7). Bake the potatoes
for 1 hour, turning
once, until tender.
2. Leave the potatoes to
cool slightly, then cut in
half and scoop out the
insides, leaving about
1 cm (1/2 inch) of
potato inside the skin.
Let the skins cool
completely, then cut
each one in half again.
3. To make the chilli
con queso, melt the
butter in a pan, add the
spring onion, chilli and
garlic and stir over low
heat for 1–2 minutes,
or until soft. Remove
from the heat and add
the sour cream and
Cheddar. Return to the
heat and stir until the
mixture is smooth.
4. Half fill a pan with
the oil and deep-fry the
skins in batches until
crisp and golden. Drain
on paper towels. Fill
with the chilli con
queso and serve with
Fresh Tomato Salsa
(page 9) and
Guacamole (page 60).

NUTRITION PER SERVE
*Protein 25 g; Fat 50 g;
Carbohydrate 35 g; Dietary
Fibre 4 g; Cholesterol
140 mg; 2700 kJ (650 cal)*

*Red-Hot Ribs (top) and
Potato Skins with Chilli Con Queso*

Chicken Tamales

Preparation time:
  45 minutes
Total cooking time:
  1 hour 20 minutes
Serves 4

Dough
100 g (3¹/₂ oz) butter, softened
1 clove garlic, crushed
1 teaspoon ground cumin
1 teaspoon salt
1¹/₂ cups (210 g/7 oz) masa harina
¹/₃ cup (80 ml/ 2³/₄ fl oz) cream
¹/₃ cup (80 ml/ 2³/₄ fl oz) chicken stock

36 corn husks or pieces of baking paper

Filling
1 corn cob
2 tablespoons oil
150 g (5 oz) chicken breast fillet
2 cloves garlic, crushed
1 red chilli, seeded and chopped
1 red onion, chopped
1 red capsicum, chopped
2 tomatoes, peeled and chopped
1 teaspoon salt

1. To make the dough, use electric beaters to beat the butter until creamy. Add the garlic, cumin and salt and mix well. Then add the masa harina and combined cream and stock alternately, and beat until smooth.
2. To make the filling, add the corn to a pan of boiling water and cook for 5–8 minutes, or until tender. Cool, then cut off the kernels. Heat the oil in a frying pan and cook the chicken until golden. Remove, cool and shred with a fork. Add the garlic, chilli and onion to the pan and cook until soft. Add the capsicum and corn and stir for 3 minutes. Add the chicken, tomato and salt and simmer for 15 minutes, or until the liquid has reduced.
3. Place the corn husks in a heatproof bowl. Cover with boiling water for 30 seconds, remove and drain. Spread a layer of dough over 12 of the husks, leaving a border at each end, then place each husk inside another. Place some filling on top and roll up. Place another husk on top to enclose if necessary and secure the ends with string. Place in a steamer to cook for 35–40 minutes. Serve with Fresh Tomato Salsa (page 9).

NUTRITION PER SERVE
Protein 15 g; Fat 40 g; Carbohydrate 50 g; Dietary Fibre 5 g; Cholesterol 110 mg; 2680 kJ (640 cal)

Chicken Tamales

Remove the kernels from the corn cob by slicing downwards with a sharp knife.

Cover the corn husks with boiling water for 30 seconds to soften.

Spread a layer of the dough over 12 of the corn husks.

Place the chicken filling over the dough and roll up the husks.

Texan Beef Chilli

Preparation time:
  15 minutes
Total cooking time:
  2 hours 15 minutes
Serves 4–6

2 kg (4 lb) chuck steak
plain flour, to coat
3 tablespoons oil
2 onions, chopped
4 cloves garlic, crushed
2 tablespoons ground
  cumin
1 tablespoon chilli
  powder
3 cups (750 ml/24 fl oz)
  beef stock

1. Trim the meat of fat and sinew, and cut into small cubes. Toss in the flour until coated, then shake off the excess.
2. Heat the oil in a large heavy-based pan. Cook the meat in batches over moderate heat until browned, then remove. Add the onion and cook, stirring occasionally, until soft and golden.
3. Add the garlic, cumin and chilli powder and cook, stirring continuously, for 1 minute. Return the meat to the pan and add the stock, stirring to scrape up the spices and juices from the bottom of the pan.
4. Bring to the boil, reduce the heat to very low and cook, covered, for 1 1/2 hours, or until the meat is tender. Stir occasionally, scraping the bottom of the pan. Remove the lid and cook for 30 minutes, or until the sauce is thick. Serve with rice.

NUTRITION PER SERVE (6)
Protein 70 g; Fat 20 g; Carbohydrate 5 g; Dietary Fibre 1 g; Cholesterol 220 mg; 1980 kJ (470 cal)

Empanadas

Preparation time:
  30 minutes + cooling
Total cooking time:
  1 hour
Makes 24

1 tablespoon oil
1 small onion, finely
  chopped
1 small green capsicum,
  finely chopped
1 clove garlic, crushed
350 g (11 1/4 oz) beef
  mince
200 g (6 1/2 oz) pork
  mince
1/2 cup (125 ml/ 4 fl oz)
  tomato purée
2 tablespoons tomato
  paste
1/2 cup (110 g/3 3/4 oz)
  chopped green olives
1/4 cup (60 ml/2 fl oz)
  dry sherry
8 frozen shortcrust
  pastry sheets, thawed
oil, for frying

1. Heat the oil in a frying pan and cook the onion for 3 minutes, or until soft. Add the capsicum, cook for 3 minutes, then add the garlic and cook for 1 minute. Add the meat and cook, breaking up any lumps with a fork, until browned.
2. Stir in the tomato purée, tomato paste, green olives and sherry and bring to the boil. Reduce the heat and simmer for 10 minutes, stirring occasionally, or until most of the liquid has evaporated. Season to taste and leave to cool completely.
3. Cut three 12 cm (5 inch) rounds from each sheet of pastry. Place a heaped tablespoon of the filling onto each round and fold over to enclose. Press the edges down with a fork to seal.
4. Heat 2 cm (3/4 inch) of the oil in a deep frying pan to moderately hot. Cook the empanadas in batches until crisp and golden brown, then drain well on paper towels. Alternatively, bake in a moderately hot 200°C (400°F/ Gas 6) oven for about 20–25 minutes.

NUTRITION PER EMPANADA
Protein 10 g; Fat 25 g; Carbohydrate 20 g; Dietary Fibre 1 g; Cholesterol 60 mg; 950 kJ (225 cal)

Texan Beef Chilli (top) with Empanadas

Coriander Tuna with Mango Salsa

Preparation time:
 25 minutes
 + marinating
Total cooking time:
 15 minutes
Serves 4

1 cup (30 g/1 oz) fresh
 coriander leaves
2 small red chillies,
 seeded and chopped
4 cloves garlic, chopped
3 cm (1¹/4 inch) piece
 fresh ginger, finely
 chopped
2 tablespoons olive oil
4 tuna steaks, about
 175 g (6 oz) each

Mango Salsa
1 mango
1 small red onion,
 finely sliced
¹/2 cup (15 g/¹/2 oz)
 fresh coriander, finely
 chopped
2 tablespoons lime juice

1. Place the coriander,
chilli, garlic, ginger and
oil in a food processor
or pestle and mortar
and process until it
forms a paste. Spread
in a thin coating over
both sides of the tuna
and marinate, covered,
in the refrigerator for
1–2 hours.
2. To make the mango
salsa, peel the mango
and cut into small
cubes. Combine with
the onion, coriander
and lime juice.
Marinate, covered,
for 20 minutes.
3. Brush a chargrill pan
lightly with a little oil
and heat until the pan
starts to smoke. Cook
the tuna for about
3–4 minutes each side
for a medium-rare pink
centre. If you prefer
your tuna well done,
cook for another
2–3 minutes each side.
Serve with the salsa.

NUTRITION PER SERVE
*Protein 12 g; Fat 11 g;
Carbohydrate 7 g; Dietary
Fibre 2 g; Cholesterol
40 mg; 740 kJ (180 cal)*

Crab Cakes with Chilli Mayonnaise

Preparation time:
 30 minutes + 1 hour
 refrigeration
Total cooking time:
 15 minutes
Serves 4

425 g (13¹/2 oz) fresh
 crab meat
1 cup (80 g/2³/4 oz)
 fresh breadcrumbs
2 spring onions, finely
 chopped
¹/2 cup (15 g/¹/2 oz)
 fresh coriander leaves,
 finely chopped
2 eggs, lightly beaten
¹/2 cup (75 g/2¹/2 oz)
 cornmeal
oil, for shallow-frying

Chilli Mayonnaise
1 egg yolk
¹/2 teaspoon Dijon
 mustard
1 teaspoon white wine
 vinegar
¹/2 cup (125 ml/4 fl oz)
 chilli oil

1. Mix the crab with
the breadcrumbs, spring
onion, coriander and
egg. Make into 8 patties.
2. Spread the cornmeal
on a plate and coat
each cake. Shake off
any excess, place on a
plate in a single layer,
cover and refrigerate
for 1 hour.
3. To make the chilli
mayonnaise, combine
the egg yolk, mustard
and vinegar and beat
for 1 minute, or until
light and creamy. Add
the oil slowly, whisking
continuously. Season,
cover and refrigerate.
4. Heat 5 mm (¹/4 inch)
of oil in a frying pan.
Cook the cakes in
batches for 3–4 minutes
on each side, or until
golden. Drain on paper
towels and serve with
the chilli mayonnaise.

NUTRITION PER SERVE
*Protein 20 g; Fat 35 g;
Carbohydrate 30 g; Dietary
Fibre 1 g; Cholesterol
225 mg; 520 kJ (30 cal)*

Note: If fresh crab isn't
available, use five 170 g
(5¹/2 oz) cans, drained.

---

*Coriander Tuna with Mango Salsa (top) and
Crab Cakes with Chilli Mayonnaise*

Baked Snapper Yucatecan

Preparation time:
  10 minutes
Total cooking time:
  35 minutes
Serves 4–6

2 snapper or bream,
  about 1 kg (2 lb) total,
  cleaned and scaled
2 tablespoons lime juice
20 g (³/4 oz) butter
1 tablespoon olive oil
1 small red capsicum,
  chopped
1 small green capsicum,
  chopped
¹/2 red onion, finely
  chopped
1 teaspoon cumin seeds
1 teaspoon grated
  orange rind
1 tablespoon chopped
  fresh coriander leaves
50 g (1³/4 oz) pepitas,
  toasted and chopped
¹/3 cup (80 ml/
  2³/4 fl oz) orange juice
1 lime, cut into wedges,
  to garnish

1. Preheat the oven to
moderate 180°C
(350°F/Gas 4). Loosely
cover the base of a
large baking dish with
a piece of aluminium
foil and lightly grease
the centre.
2. Rub the fish inside
and out with the lime
juice and season with
salt and black pepper.
Place in the centre of
the foil, then pull the
sides up to form a
bowl shape.
3. Heat the butter and
olive oil in a pan and
add the red and green
capsicum, onion, cumin
seeds and orange rind
and cook over medium
heat, stirring, for about
2 minutes. Stir in the
coriander and pepitas
and season to taste.
Spread this mixture
over the fish and pour
the orange juice over
the top. Loosely cover
with foil, folding the
sides of the 2 sheets
together to seal.
4. Bake for 30 minutes,
or until the flesh of the
fish flakes easily when
tested with a fork at the
thickest part. Remove
the foil and transfer to
a serving platter. Spoon
the juices over the fish
to moisten. Garnish
with the lime wedges
to serve.

NUTRITION PER SERVE (6)
*Protein 40 g; Fat 20 g;
Carbohydrate 5 g; Dietary
Fibre 2 g; Cholesterol
130 mg; 1390 kJ (330 cal)*

Note: For a special
occasion, you can wrap
the fish in banana
leaves instead of foil
to give a lovely flavour
to this dish and an
interesting appearance.

Corn and Sweet Potato Pudding

Preparation time:
  20 minutes
Total cooking time:
  1 hour
Serves 4–6

1¹/2 tablespoons olive
  oil
1 onion, grated
375 g (12 oz) can
  creamed corn
¹/2 cup (125 g/4 oz)
  cooked and mashed
  sweet potato
¹/2 cup (125 ml/4 fl oz)
  milk
¹/2 cup (125 ml/4 fl oz)
  cream
3 eggs, lightly beaten
1 teaspoon salt

1. Preheat the oven to
moderate 180°C
(350°F/Gas 4). Heat the
oil in a frying pan. Fry
the onion until soft and
place in a large bowl.
2. Stir in the remaining
ingredients to combine.
3. Pour the mixture
into a lightly greased
1 litre capacity
ovenproof dish and
bake for 45 minutes–
1 hour, or until puffed
and golden. Serve with
a salad and bread or as
an accompaniment to
meat dishes.

NUTRITION PER SERVE (6)
*Protein 6 g; Fat 14 g;
Carbohydrate 16 g; Dietary
Fibre 3 g; Cholesterol
120 mg; 880 kJ (210 cal)*

*Baked Snapper Yucatecan (top) with
Corn and Sweet Potato Pudding*

FLOUR TORTILLAS

CORN TORTILLAS

Tex-Mex Breads and Chips

A Tex-Mex meal usually includes tortillas or breads. You can buy them ready-made for a quick meal, or make your own for a special occasion. Guacamole is the perfect accompaniment for corn chips.

Flour Tortillas

Sift 3 cups (375 g/ 12 oz) plain flour and 1 teaspoon salt into a large bowl and make a well in the centre. Using a flat-bladed knife, mix in $^1/3$ cup (80 ml/ $2^3/4$ fl oz) oil and up to 1 cup (250 ml/8 fl oz) warm water until a soft dough forms. Place on an unfloured board and knead for 5 minutes, or until smooth and elastic. Put in a clean bowl, cover and place in a warm place for 1 hour. Divide the dough into 12 pieces, roll into balls and flatten and place on a lightly floured work surface. Roll each ball into a 20 cm (8 inch) circle and place in a stack covered by a layer of plastic wrap. Heat a heavy-based or cast-iron frying pan over medium heat. Place a tortilla in the pan and cook for 1 minute. If it puffs up, gently push it down. Turn over, cook for 1 minute, then serve. To store, cool, then stack on top of each other. The tortillas can be wrapped in foil when cold, then frozen. Reheat in the oven, microwave or a pan. Makes 12 tortillas.

NUTRITION PER TORTILLA
Protein 3 g; Fat 7 g; Carbohydrate 23 g; Dietary Fibre 1 g; Cholesterol 0 mg; 695 kJ (165 cal)

Corn Tortillas

Place 3 cups (435 g/ 14 oz) masa harina in a large bowl. Add $1^3/4$ cups (440 ml/ 14 fl oz) warm water. Using your hands, mix until the dough comes together to form a ball. Divide into 12 pieces and roll into balls. Flatten and place each ball between 2 layers of plastic wrap. Roll out to 18 cm (7 inch) rounds, trimming the edges to make neat circles. Cover, as the mixture drys out very easily. Heat a heavy-based or cast-iron frying pan over medium heat. Place a tortilla in the pan and cook for

1 minute. Turn over and cook for 1 minute. Turn again to the first side and cook for another 30 seconds, or until the tortilla puffs slightly but is still pliable. Remove and repeat with the remaining tortillas. Makes 12 tortillas.

NUTRITION PER TORTILLA
Protein 3 g; Fat 0 g; Carbohydrate 26 g; Dietary Fibre 1 g; Cholesterol 0 mg; 520 kJ (125 cal)

Variation: To make blue corn tortillas, use blue masa harina.

Cornbread

Preheat the oven to hot 220°C (425°F/Gas 7). Generously brush a 20 cm (8 inch) cast-iron pan (with an ovenproof or screw-off handle) or cake tin with corn oil. Place in the oven to heat while making the batter.

Combine 1 cup (150 g/5 oz) cornmeal, 1 cup (125 g/4 oz) self-raising flour and 1 teaspoon salt in a bowl and make a well in the centre. Whisk together 1 egg, 1 cup (250 ml/8 fl oz) buttermilk and 1/4 cup (60 ml/2 fl oz) oil, pour into the dry ingredients and stir until just combined, taking care not to overbeat. Pour into the pan, and bake for 25 minutes, or until lightly brown and firm. Cut into 8 wedges.

NUTRITION PER WEDGE
Protein 4 g; Fat 9 g; Carbohydrate 30 g; Dietary Fibre 1 g; Cholesterol 25 mg; 935 kJ (220 cal

Corn Chips

Prepare 1 quantity of blue or white corn tortillas up to the stage just before cooking. Cut each tortilla into 8 wedges, split in half

and allow to dry for 1 hour. Use enough corn or vegetable oil to half fill a large deep pan or deep-fryer and heat to about 190°C (375°F). Working in batches, fry the corn chips, stirring once or twice, for 1 minute, or until crisp but not brown. Remove with a slotted spoon, drain on paper towels and sprinkle with salt. The corn chips can be stored in an airtight container for a day. To reheat, put inside a paper bag and place in a warm oven for 10 minutes. Serves 4–6.

NUTRITION PER SERVE
Protein 3 g; Fat 13 g; Carbohydrate 25 g; Dietary Fibre 1 g; Cholesterol 0 mg; 990 kJ (235 cal)

Note: Serve 1 quantity of blue and 1 quantity of white corn chips together in a bowl for a great effect.

Beef Picadillo

Preparation time:
  10 minutes
Total cooking time:
  1 hour
Serves 4–6

1 onion, finely chopped
2 cloves garlic, crushed
750 g (1¹/₂ lb) beef
  mince
3 tablespoons dry sherry
3 tablespoons lime juice
2 tomatoes, peeled,
  seeded and chopped
1 tablespoon tomato
  paste
3 green serrano chillies,
  seeded and chopped
75 g (2¹/₂ oz) stuffed
  green olives, sliced
2 tablespoons capers
2 tablespoons sultanas
¹/₂ cup (125 ml/4 fl oz)
  beef stock
1 potato, cut into cubes
1 choko or zucchini,
  cut into cubes
1 teaspoon ground
  cumin

1. Heat some oil in a
pan and stir the onion
for 5 minutes, or until
golden. Add the garlic,
stir for 1 minute, then
add the beef. Increase
the heat and cook,
stirring occasionally,
for 10 minutes. Reduce
the heat, add the sherry
and lime juice and cook
for 5 minutes, then add
the tomato, tomato
paste, 2 chillies, olives,
capers, sultanas and

stock. Cover and
simmer for 20 minutes.
2. Heat some oil in a
pan, add the potato,
choko or zucchini and
cumin. Stir until brown,
then cook gently for
10 minutes. Add to the
beef mixture and cook
for 5 minutes. Top with
the remaining chilli and
serve with Flour
Tortillas (page 22).

NUTRITION PER SERVE (6)
*Protein 30 g; Fat 15 g;
Carbohydrate 7 g; Dietary
Fibre 3 g; Cholesterol
80 mg; 1170 kJ (300 cal)*

Corn Dogs with Jalapeño Salsa

Preparation time:
  30 minutes +
  10 minutes standing
Total cooking time:
  35 minutes
Serves 8

³/₄ cup (110 g/3³/₄ oz)
  coarse cornmeal
2 tablespoons sugar
1 egg
¹/₂ cup (125 ml/4 fl oz)
  milk
60 g (2 oz) butter, melted
1 cup (125 g/4 oz) plain
  flour
1¹/₂ teaspoons baking
  powder
oil, for deep-frying
16 continental hot dogs
16 wooden skewers
plain flour, for coating

Salsa
3–4 jalapeño chillies,
  seeded and chopped
2 cloves garlic, crushed
²/₃ cup (45 g/1¹/₂ oz)
  chopped spring onion
8 large tomatoes, diced
2 tablespoons lime juice
2 tablespoons chopped
  fresh coriander

1. Combine the
cornmeal, 1 teaspoon
salt, sugar and ³/₄ cup
(185 ml/6 fl oz) boiling
water. Cover and leave
for 10 minutes. Stir the
egg, milk and butter
into the cornmeal, then
sift in the flour and
baking powder and stir.
2. To make the salsa,
heat some oil in a pan
and fry the chilli, garlic
and spring onion for
1 minute. Add the
tomato, cover and
simmer for 20 minutes.
Add the lime juice
and coriander.
3. Heat the oil to 190°C
(375°F). Insert a skewer
into each hot dog. Place
the flour on baking
paper and coat the hot
dogs, then dip into the
cornmeal mixture.
Lower into the oil, 3 at
a time, turning until
golden. Drain, then serve
with the warm salsa.

NUTRITION PER SERVE
*Protein 20 g; Fat 40 g;
Carbohydrate 30 g; Dietary
Fibre 6 g; Cholesterol
100 mg; 2300 kJ (550 cal)*

*Beef Picadillo (top) and
Corn Dogs with Jalapeño Salsa*

Texan Chilli Burgers

Preparation time:
 25 minutes
Total cooking time:
 40 minutes
Serves 4

Burgers
*3 teaspoons ground
 cumin
1 teaspoon ground
 coriander
1 kg (2 lb) beef mince
1 onion, finely chopped
1 cup (80 g/2³/4 oz)
 fresh breadcrumbs
1 egg, lightly beaten
2 chillies, seeded and
 chopped
2 cloves garlic, crushed*

Sweet Onion Relish
*1 tablespoon oil
2 large onions, finely
 sliced
¹/4 cup (55 g/1³/4 oz)
 firmly packed soft
 brown sugar
1 tablespoon malt
 vinegar*

*4 hamburger buns or
 bread rolls*

1. To make the burgers,
put the cumin and
coriander into a dry
frying pan and stir over
low heat for about
1 minute, or until
fragrant. Combine with
all the remaining
burger ingredients in a
bowl, using your hands
to mix thoroughly.
Divide the mixture into
4 and shape into patties
2 cm (³/4 inch) thick.
2. To make the relish,
heat the oil in a pan,
add the onion and cook
over moderate heat,
stirring occasionally,
for 10 minutes, or until
golden brown and soft.
Stir in the brown sugar
and malt vinegar and
cook for a further
10 minutes, stirring
occasionally. Season.
3. Brush a barbecue or
frying pan lightly with
oil and heat to
moderately hot. Cook
the burgers for about
8 minutes on each side,
turning only once
during cooking. Split
the hamburger buns
and toast the insides.
Serve the burgers on
the buns or bread rolls,
with some lettuce
leaves, tomato slices,
the sweet onion relish
and a spoonful of
sour cream.

NUTRITION PER SERVE
*Protein 60 g; Fat 35 g;
Carbohydrate 55 g; Dietary
Fibre 5 g; Cholesterol
200 mg; 3295 kJ (785 cal)*

Note: This recipe
makes very large
burgers. Divide the
mixture into 6 for
medium burgers.

Tex-Mex Roasted Chicken

Preparation time:
 20 minutes
Total cooking time:
 50 minutes
Serves 4

*2 x 1 kg (2 lb) chickens,
 washed and dried
3 tablespoons olive oil
4 cloves garlic, crushed
1 tablespoon ground
 cumin
1 tablespoon ground
 coriander
1 tablespoon New
 Mexico chilli powder
 or mild chilli powder
1 teaspoon ground
 cinnamon
1 tablespoon plain flour*

1. Preheat the oven to
moderately hot 200°C
(400°F/Gas 6). Cut the
chickens in half with
scissors or a knife.
Combine the oil and
garlic and brush both
inside and outside.
2. Combine the spices
and flour in a bowl.
Coat the chicken lightly
and place on a rack in a
baking dish. Drizzle
with a little oil and
bake for about
45–50 minutes. Stand
for 5 minutes, then
serve with lime wedges.

NUTRITION PER SERVE
*Protein 110 g; Fat 25 g;
Carbohydrate 2 g; Dietary
Fibre 0 g; Cholesterol
250 mg; 2920 kJ (700 cal)*

*Texan Chilli Burgers (top) with
Tex-Mex Roasted Chicken*

Chicken Tacos

Preparation time:
  20 minutes
Total cooking time:
  15 minutes
Serves 4

1 onion, finely chopped
2 cloves garlic, crushed
3 tomatoes, chopped
1 chilli, seeded and
  chopped
1 teaspoon sugar
1 barbecue chicken
8 large taco shells
4 lettuce leaves, shredded
1¹/2 cups (185 g/6 oz)
  grated Cheddar

1. Preheat the oven to
moderate 180°C
(350°F/Gas 4). Heat
some oil and cook the
onion for 3 minutes.
Add the garlic and
cook for 1 minute. Add
the tomato, chilli and
sugar, bring to the boil,
reduce the heat and
simmer for 5 minutes,
or until thick. Season.
2. Remove the meat
from the chicken and
shred, using 2 forks to
pull apart. Stir into the
sauce. Heat the taco
shells in the oven for
5 minutes.
3. To serve, fill the
tacos with the chicken,
lettuce and cheese.

NUTRITION PER SERVE
*Protein 14 g; Fat 22 g;
Carbohydrate 6 g; Dietary
Fibre 3 g; Cholesterol
50 mg; 1430 kJ (330 cal)*

Seafood Burritos

Preparation time:
  45 minutes
Total cooking time:
  40 minutes
Serves 4

¹/3 cup (80 ml/
  2³/4 fl oz) oil
70 g (2¹/4 oz) butter
2 cloves garlic, crushed
3 small red chillies,
  seeded and chopped
250 g (8 oz) scallops,
  cleaned
500 g (1 lb) medium
  raw prawns, shelled
  and deveined
500 g (1 lb) salmon
  fillet, cut into small
  pieces
4 flour tortillas (ready-
  made or see page 22)
2¹/2 tablespoons plain
  flour
¹/2 cup (125 ml/4 fl oz)
  cream
³/4 cup (185 ml/6 fl oz)
  milk
¹/2 cup (125 g/4 oz)
  sour cream
¹/3 cup (35 g/1¹/4 oz)
  grated Parmesan
2 tablespoons chopped
  fresh parsley
1 cup (125 g/4 oz)
  grated Cheddar

1. Preheat the oven to
warm 160°C (315°F/
Gas 2–3). Heat the oil
and 30 g (1 oz) of the
butter in a frying pan.
Add the garlic and

chilli and cook for
1 minute. Add the
scallops and cook for
2–3 minutes, then
remove and drain on
paper towels. Add the
prawns and cook for
2–3 minutes; drain on
paper towels. Add the
salmon, cook for
3–4 minutes, then
remove and drain on
paper towels. Place all
the seafood in a bowl.
2. Wrap the tortillas in
foil and place in the
oven for 10 minutes to
warm. In a pan, melt
the remaining butter,
add the flour and stir
until the mixture begins
to froth. Remove from
the heat and gradually
stir in the cream and
milk. Return to the
heat and whisk until
the sauce thickens and
boils. Stir in the sour
cream, Parmesan and
parsley, pour over the
seafood and mix well.
3. Fill each tortilla with
the seafood and roll up.
Place in a lightly
greased ovenproof dish,
sprinkle over the cheese
and bake for about
15–20 minutes, or until
heated through and the
cheese has melted.
Serve on hot Red Chilli
Sauce (page 38).

NUTRITION PER SERVE
*Protein 80 g; Fat 90 g;
Carbohydrate 30 g; Dietary
Fibre 2 g; Cholesterol 440
mg; 5080 kJ (1215 cal)*

Chicken Tacos (top) with Seafood Burritos

Remove the seeds from the chillies, using rubber gloves to protect your hands.

Add the steak to the onion and spices and turn with tongs to coat well.

Beef Chimichangas

Preparation time:
  30 minutes
Total cooking time:
  2 hours 50 minutes
Serves 4

2 tablespoons oil
1 large onion, finely
  chopped
1 clove garlic, crushed
2 teaspoons ground
  cumin
fi teaspoon ground
  cinnamon
2 chillies, seeded and
  chopped
1 kg (2 lb) rump steak
2 cups (500 ml/16 fl oz)
  beef stock
4 flour tortillas
  (ready-made or see
  page 22)
oil, for frying

1. Heat the oil in a large pan and cook the onion over medium heat for 10 minutes, or until very soft and golden brown. Add the garlic, cumin, cinnamon and chilli and cook, stirring, for another minute.
2. Add the steak and turn to coat with the spices, then stir in the stock, scraping the bottom of the pan. Bring just to the boil, reduce the heat and gently simmer, covered, for 1 hour. Uncover and cook for a further 1–1¹/2 hours, or until the liquid has just about evaporated. Stir frequently towards the end of the cooking time to prevent burning on the bottom of the pan.
3. Shred the meat, using 2 forks to pull it apart, then leave to cool.
4. Preheat the oven to warm 160°C (315°F/ Gas 2–3). Wrap the tortillas in foil and place in the oven for 10 minutes to soften. Remove from the oven and leave wrapped for another 5 minutes. Working with one at a time (and leaving the other tortillas wrapped as you work), place a quarter of the meat on one tortilla, and fold in the sides to enclose. Set aside, fold-side-down, while you fill the remaining tortillas.
5. Heat about 2 cm (³/4 inch) of oil in a frying pan to moderately hot. Place a few chimichangas fold-side-down in the pan, then turn and cook the other side until golden and crisp. Repeat with the rest of the chimichangas. Drain on paper towels. Serve immediately with some Red Chilli Sauce (page 38) and Mexican Rice (page 63).

NUTRITION PER SERVE
Protein 60 g; Fat 20 g; Carbohydrate 20 g; Dietary Fibre 2 g; Cholesterol 170 mg; 2240 kJ (535 cal)

Beef Chimichangas

Shred the beef, using 2 forks to pull the meat apart.

Place a quarter of the meat onto each tortilla and fold in the sides to enclose.

Bean Tostadas

Preparation time:
  30 minutes
Total cooking time:
  15 minutes
Serves 4

2 tomatoes, chopped
1 small red onion,
  finely chopped
1 small red chilli, finely
  chopped
3 tablespoons finely
  chopped fresh
  coriander
2 tablespoons oil
4 corn tortillas (ready-
  made or see page 22)
450 g (14¹/4 oz)
  Refried Beans (ready-
  made or see page 63)
4 lettuce leaves,
  shredded
1 cup (125 g/4 oz)
  grated Cheddar
1 avocado, sliced
¹/3 cup (90 g/3 oz) sour
  cream
sliced black olives, to
  garnish

1. Combine the tomato,
onion, chilli and
coriander in a bowl,
cover and set aside.
Heat the oil in a heavy-
based frying pan and
cook the tortillas, one
at a time, for 1–2
minutes on each side,
or until crisp. Drain on
paper towels. Warm the
refried beans in a pan.
2. To assemble, spread
each tortilla with the
refried beans, then top
with the lettuce, tomato
mixture and Cheddar.
Arrange the avocado,
sour cream and olives
on top.

NUTRITION PER SERVE
*Protein 10 g; Fat 50 g;
Carbohydrate 15 g; Dietary
Fibre 10 g; Cholesterol
30 mg; 2270 kJ (540 cal)*

Chicken Enchiladas

Preparation time:
  40 minutes
Total cooking time:
  1 hour 10 minutes
Serves 4

2 large red chillies
2 large green chillies
1 tablespoon oil
1 onion, finely chopped
2 cloves garlic, crushed
1 cup (250 ml/8 fl oz)
  chicken stock
1 cup (250 ml/8 fl oz)
  tomato purée
1 barbecue chicken
8 corn tortillas (ready-
  made or see page 22)
1 cup (125 g/4 oz)
  grated Cheddar

1. Roast the chillies by
holding with tongs one
at a time in a gas flame,
or flatten out and cook
under a hot grill, until
the skins are black and
blistered. Cool in a
plastic bag, then peel,
discard the seeds and
chop finely.
2. Heat the oil in a pan
and add the onion.
Cook over low heat for
5 minutes, or until the
onion is soft. Add the
garlic and cook for
1 more minute. Add the
chillies, stock and
tomato purée, bring to
the boil, reduce the
heat and simmer for
15 minutes. Season
with salt and pepper.
3. Preheat the oven to
moderate 180°C
(350°F/Gas 4).Remove
the meat from the
chicken and shred
finely, using 2 forks to
pull the meat apart.
Heat a little oil in a
heavy-based frying pan
and cook the tortillas,
1 at a time, for about
1 minute each side, or
until soft and warm but
not crisp. Drain on
paper towels.
4. Spread ¹/4 cup
(60 ml/2 fl oz) of the
sauce into the bottom
of a large baking dish.
Fill the tortillas with
the chicken and roll
up. Arrange in the dish
and pour over the
remaining sauce and
the Cheddar. Bake for
20 minutes, or until the
enchiladas are cooked
through and the cheese
has melted.

NUTRITION PER SERVE
*Protein 40 g; Fat 40 g;
Carbohydrate 8 g; Dietary
Fibre 3 g; Cholesterol
165 mg; 2250 kJ (535 cal)*

Bean Tostadas (top) with Chicken Enchiladas

Chilli Con Carne

Preparation time:
  20 minutes
Total cooking time:
  1 hour 20 minutes
Serves 4–6

1 tablespoon oil
1 large onion, chopped
2 cloves garlic, crushed
1 teaspoon chilli
  powder
1 tablespoon ground
  cumin
1 kg (2 lb) beef mince
400 g (12³/4 oz) can
  crushed tomatoes
1 cup (250 ml/8 fl oz)
  beef stock
1 teaspoon dried
  oregano
2 teaspoons sugar
2 tablespoons tomato
  paste
400 g (12³/4 oz) can
  red kidney beans,
  rinsed and drained

1. Heat the oil in a large pan and add the onion. Cook over medium heat for 5 minutes, or until soft and golden. Add the garlic, chilli and cumin, and cook for 1 minute.
2. Add the meat and cook for 5 minutes, or until browned, breaking up any lumps with a fork as it cooks.
3. Stir in the tomato, stock, oregano and sugar. Bring to the boil, reduce the heat and simmer, partially covered, for 1 hour, stirring occasionally.
4. Stir in the tomato paste and beans and season. Cook for 5 minutes to heat the beans, then serve with cornbread to mop up the juices.

NUTRITION PER SERVE (6)
Protein 40 g; Fat 20 g; Carbohydrate 15 g; Dietary Fibre 6 g; Cholesterol 100 mg; 1700 kJ (405 cal)

Cornbread with Chillies and Cheese

Preparation time:
  30 minutes
Total cooking time:
  1 hour
Serves 4–6

1 small red capsicum
2 long red chillies
2 long green chillies
¹/2 cup (60 g/2 oz)
  grated Cheddar
2 cups (300 g/10 oz)
  fine cornmeal
¹/3 cup (90 g/3 oz)
  sugar
2 teaspoons baking
  powder
1 teaspoon bicarbonate
  of soda
420 g (13¹/2 oz) can
  creamed corn
¹/2 cup (125 ml/4 fl oz)
  buttermilk
1 cup (125 g/4 oz)
  grated Cheddar, extra

1. Preheat the oven to moderately hot 190°C (375°F/Gas 5). Grease a 1.75 litre capacity ovenproof dish.
2. Cut the capsicum into quarters and remove the seeds and membrane. Place the capsicum and chillies under a preheated grill and cook until the skins blister and blacken. Remove from the grill, place in a plastic bag to cool, then peel. Remove the seeds and membrane from the chillies and cut the capsicum and chillies into fine strips.
3. Combine the Cheddar, cornmeal, sugar, baking powder and bicarbonate of soda in a bowl and mix well. Add the creamed corn, buttermilk and the chilli and capsicum strips and mix gently until combined. Spoon into the dish and smooth the top with the back of the spoon. Sprinkle with the extra Cheddar and bake for 40 minutes, or until the cornbread has risen and is set in the centre.

NUTRITION PER SERVE (6)
Protein 10 g; Fat 12 g; Carbohydrate 70 g; Dietary Fibre 3 g; Cholesterol 35 mg; 1785 kJ (425 cal)

*Chilli Con Carne (top) and
Cornbread with Chillies and Cheese*

Chicken Mole

Preparation time:
1 hour + 35 minutes
soaking
Total cooking time:
2 hours
Serves 4–6

1.6 kg (3 lb 4 oz)
  chicken
6 cloves garlic
2 onions, chopped
50 g (1³/4 oz) mulato
  chillies
60 g (2 oz) pasilla
  chillies
60 g (2 oz) ancho
  chillies
3 whole cloves
3 whole allspice
2 teaspoons dried
  thyme
2 teaspoons dried
  marjoram
2 teaspoons dried
  oregano
¹/4 cup (40 g/1¹/4 oz)
  sesame seeds
¹/4 cup (40 g/1¹/4 oz)
  unsalted peanuts
8 almonds
2 tablespoons raisins
3 cinnamon sticks,
  slivered
90 g (3 oz) Mexican
  drinking chocolate or
  bittersweet chocolate

1. Preheat the oven to moderately hot 190°C (375°F/Gas 5). Cut the chicken into 8 pieces, wash and rinse well. Place in a pan with 4 cloves garlic and half the onion. Pour in enough water to cover completely, bring to the boil, reduce the heat to a simmer and cook for 30 minutes, or until just tender. Remove the chicken and strain the stock, reserving just over 1 litre.

2. Cut the chillies open and remove and reserve the seeds. Bake the chillies for 5 minutes, then place in a dish, cover with water and soak for 30 minutes.

3. Place the chilli seeds in a dry frying pan. Cook over medium heat, shaking to brown evenly. Once browned, increase the heat and char until black. Place in a bowl, cover with water and soak for 5 minutes. Drain the seeds and place in a blender or food processor with ²/3 cup (170 ml/5¹/2 fl oz) water, the cloves, allspice, thyme, marjoram and oregano.

4. Heat 1 tablespoon of oil in a heavy-based pan. Add the sesame seeds and fry until dark brown. Add to the blender or food processor, leaving any extra oil in the pan. Blend well.

5. Heat another tablespoon of oil. Add the peanuts, almonds and raisins and cook until the nuts are golden and the raisins puff up, stirring constantly. Place in the blender. Add the remaining onion and garlic and the cinnamon to the pan, cook until golden, then add to the blender. Blend until the mixture is a thick paste, adding a little water if necessary. Heat some oil in a pan, add the paste and fry for 15 minutes, scraping the pan occasionally.

6. Place half the chillies in the clean blender with 125 ml (4 fl oz) of the chilli soaking liquid and blend until smooth, adding more liquid if the mixture becomes too thick. Add the remaining chillies and more liquid and blend until smooth. Add to the pan with the chocolate, mix well and simmer for 5 minutes. Add 1 litre of the stock and stir until well combined. Bring to the boil and simmer for 35 minutes. Add the chicken, season with salt to taste and cook for about 10 minutes. Add a little more stock to thin the sauce if necessary.

NUTRITION PER SERVE (6)
*Protein 75 g; Fat 50 g;
Carbohydrate 20 g; Dietary
Fibre 4 g; Cholesterol
225 mg; 3430 kJ (820 cal)*

Chicken Mole

FRESH CORN
AND TOMATO
SALSA

MIXED CAPSICUM
SALSA

PEACH AND
GINGER SALSA

Sauces and Salsas

A Tex-Mex sauce is cooked, while a salsa is a mixture of raw ingredients. Just a spoonful of sauce or salsa on the side will add extra zing to your Tex-Mex meal.

Red Chilli Sauce

Roast 2 large fresh red chillies by placing under a preheated grill or holding with tongs in an open gas flame, until the skin is black and blistered. Cool in a plastic bag, then peel the skin and remove the seeds and stem. Dry-fry 1 teaspoon ground cumin in a pan for 30 seconds, or until fragrant. Combine the chilli, cumin, 400 g (12^3/4 oz) can tomatoes, 1 small chopped red onion, 1 crushed clove garlic, ^{1}/2 cup (125 ml/ 4 fl oz) chicken stock and 2 teaspoons red wine vinegar in a food processor and blend until smooth. Transfer to a pan, bring to the boil, then reduce the heat and simmer for 20 minutes. Refrigerate, covered, for up to 2 days. Serve warm or at room temperature. Makes 1^1/2 cups (375 ml/12 fl oz).

NUTRITION PER SERVE
*Protein 1 g; Fat 0 g;
Carbohydrate 4 g; Dietary
Fibre 1.4 g; Cholesterol
0 mg; 90 kJ (20 cal)*

Green Chilli Sauce

Combine 2 large fresh green chillies, 340 g (10^3/4 oz) can drained tomatillos, 1 small onion, 1 crushed clove garlic and ^{1}/2 cup (125 ml/4 fl oz) chicken stock in a food processor and blend until smooth. Transfer to a pan and bring to the boil. Reduce the heat to medium and simmer for 10 minutes. Refrigerate, covered, for up to 2 days. Serve warm or at room temperature. Makes 1 cup (250 ml/8 fl oz).

NUTRITION PER SERVE
*Protein 2 g; Fat 0 g;
Carbohydrate 5 g; Dietary
Fibre 2 g; Cholesterol
0 mg; 125 kJ (30 cal)*

Mixed Capsicum Salsa

Finely chop 1 small red capsicum, 1 small yellow capsicum and 1 small green capsicum and place in a large mixing bowl. Add 1 finely chopped red onion, 5 finely sliced spring onions and 1/4 cup (15 g/1/2 oz) finely chopped fresh coriander. Stir in 2–3 tablespoons of lime juice, according to taste. Mix together until well combined and serve immediately. Serves 4.

NUTRITION PER SERVE
Protein 1 g; Fat 0 g; Carbohydrate 3 g; Dietary Fibre 1 g; Cholesterol 0 mg; 75 kJ (20 cal)

Fresh Corn and Tomato Salsa

Bring a large pan of salted water to the boil and cook 2 corn cobs in the boiling water until tender. Cool completely, then remove the kernels by cutting downwards with a sharp knife. Place in a large mixing bowl. Seed and finely chop 1 ripe tomato and add to the corn kernels along with 1 seeded and finely chopped green jalepeño chilli, 1 finely chopped red onion, 3 tablespoons chopped fresh coriander and 2–3 tablespoons lime juice, according to taste. Mix until well combined and serve the salsa immediately. Serves 4.

NUTRITION PER SERVE
Protein 1 g; Fat 0 g; Carbohydrate 7 g; Dietary Fibre 1 g; Cholesterol 0 mg; 50 kJ (40 cal)

Melon and Chilli Salsa

Place 2 cups (340 g/ 10 3/4 oz) finely diced honeydew melon into a bowl. Add 1 finely chopped red onion, 2 seeded and finely chopped small red chillies and 3 tablespoons finely chopped fresh coriander. Mix until well combined. Stir in 2–3 tablespoons freshly squeezed lime juice, according to taste. Serve immediately. Serves 4.

NUTRITION PER SERVE
Protein 0 g; Fat 0 g; Carbohydrate 2 g; Dietary Fibre 0 g; Cholesterol 0 mg; 55 kJ (15 cal)

Peach and Ginger Salsa

Peel and finely dice 3 ripe peaches. Place in a bowl and combine with 2 teaspoons finely grated fresh ginger, 2 tablespoons finely sliced spring onions, 3 tablespoons chopped fresh coriander and 2–3 tablespoons lime juice, according to taste. Mix until well combined and serve the salsa immediately. Serves 4.

NUTRITION PER SERVE
Protein 0 g; Fat 0 g; Carbohydrate 2 g; Dietary Fibre 0 g; Cholesterol 0 mg; 30 kJ (8 cal)

MELON AND CHILLI SALSA

RED CHILLI SAUCE

GREEN CHILLI SAUCE

Chicken Tostadas

Preparation time:
45 minutes
Total cooking time:
30 minutes
Serves 4

8 corn tortillas (ready-
made or see page 22)
oil, for deep-frying
500 g (1 lb) chicken
breast fillets
1 teaspoon pepper
$^{1}/_{2}$ teaspoon paprika
4 large lettuce leaves,
shredded
$1^{1}/_{4}$ cups (155 g/5 oz)
grated Cheddar
2 avocados, sliced
$^{1}/_{3}$ cup (90 g/3 oz) sour
cream
4 spring onions, sliced
on the diagonal

1. Preheat the oven to warm 160°C (315°F/ Gas 2–3). Wrap the tortillas in foil and place in the oven for 10 minutes to warm. Heat the oil in a deep pan. Using 2 gaufrette baskets, one smaller than the other, place 1 tortilla in the larger basket and place the smaller basket on top. Keep the other tortillas covered. Deep-fry until crisp and golden, then drain on paper towels. Repeat with the remaining tortillas.
2. Sprinkle the chicken with the pepper and paprika. Heat some oil in a frying pan and cook for 4–5 minutes each side. Cool slightly, then slice thinly.
3. Fill the tortilla baskets with the lettuce, Cheddar, chicken slices, avocado, a spoonful of sour cream, the spring onions and some Fresh Tomato Salsa (see page 9).

NUTRITION PER SERVE
*Protein 40 g; Fat 50 g;
Carbohydrate 4 g; Dietary
Fibre 3 g; Cholesterol
130 mg; 2720 kJ (650 cal)*

Seafood Fajitas

Preparation time:
30 minutes
Total cooking time:
20 minutes
Serves 2

3 ripe tomatoes, finely
chopped
1 small red chilli, finely
chopped
2 spring onions, finely
sliced
300 g (10 oz) medium
raw prawns, peeled,
deveined and halved
250 g (8 oz) scallops,
cleaned and halved
250 g (8 oz) boneless
white fish fillets, cut
into bite-size cubes
$^{1}/_{3}$ cup (80 ml/
$2^{3}/_{4}$ fl oz) lime juice
1 clove garlic, crushed
1 avocado
2 tablespoons lemon
juice
4 flour tortillas (ready-
made or see page 22)
1 onion, sliced
1 green capsicum, cut
into thin strips

1. Preheat the oven to warm 160°C (315°F/ Gas 2–3). Combine the tomato, chilli and spring onion in a bowl, then season to taste.
2. Combine the prawns, scallops, fish, lime juice and garlic in a non-metallic dish. Cover and set aside.
3. Slice the avocado and brush with the lemon juice to prevent browning. Wrap the tortillas in foil and place in the oven for 10 minutes to soften.
4. Heat a lightly oiled chargrill or cast-iron pan to very hot, add the onion and capsicum and cook, turning occasionally, until soft and lightly brown; push to one side. Drain the seafood and cook briefly until it is seared and just turns opaque.
5. To serve, wrap the seafood, capsicum, onion and the tomato mixture and the avocado in the tortillas.

NUTRITION PER SERVE
*Protein 85 g; Fat 45 g;
Carbohydrate 50 g; Dietary
Fibre 9 g; Cholesterol
350 mg; 4000 kJ (960 cal)*

Chicken Tostadas (top) with Seafood Fajitas

Cheese and Bean Nachos

Preparation time:
30 minutes
Total cooking time:
15 minutes
Serves 4

3 tomatoes, finely
  chopped
1 small red onion,
  finely chopped
3 tablespoons chopped
  fresh coriander
1 small red chilli, finely
  chopped
2 x 400 g (12³/4 oz)
  cans red kidney beans,
  rinsed and drained
2 x 230 g (7¹/4 oz)
  packets corn chips
2 cups (250 g/8 oz)
  grated Cheddar
1 large avocado
¹/3 cup (90 g/3 oz) sour
  cream
2 spring onions, finely
  sliced

1. Preheat the oven to
moderate 180°C
(350°F/Gas 4).
Combine the tomato,
onion, coriander and
chilli in a bowl. Place
the kidney beans in a
pan, cover with water
and bring to the boil.
Drain and return to the
pan. Add ¹/2 cup of the
tomato mixture and
cook for 5 minutes,
stirring often.
2. Place the bean
mixture in an
ovenproof tray and
cover with the corn
chips. Sprinkle over the
Cheddar and bake for
3–5 minutes, or until
the cheese melts.
Transfer to plates.
3. Spread the remaining
tomato mixture over
the melted cheese, then
lightly mash the
avocado and place on
top, with a spoonful of
sour cream and the
sliced spring onions.

NUTRITION PER SERVE
*Protein 40 g; Fat 80 g;
Carbohydrate 90 g; Dietary
Fibre 30 g; Cholesterol
95 mg; 1155 kJ (1230 cal)*

Beef with Black Bean Salsa

Preparation time:
30 minutes + 1 hour
30 minutes standing
Total cooking time:
1 hour 30 minutes
Serves 4–6

¹/2 cup (110 g/3³/4 oz)
  dried black beans
1 small red capsicum
1 small onion, finely
  chopped
3 cloves garlic, crushed
1 corn cob, kernels
  removed
2 tomatoes, chopped
¹/2 cup (15 g/¹/2 oz)
  chopped fresh
  coriander
3 tablespoons lime juice
4 fillet steaks

1. Place the beans in a
pan and cover with
water. Bring to the boil,
then remove from the
heat, cover and stand
for 1 hour. Drain and
rinse well. Return to
the pan, cover with
water, bring to the boil
and simmer for 1 hour,
or until tender. Drain.
2. Cut the capsicum in
quarters and remove
the seeds and membrane.
Place under a preheated
grill and cook until the
skin blisters and
blackens. Cool in a
plastic bag, then peel
and cut into strips.
3. Heat some oil in a
frying pan, cook the
onion until soft, add
the garlic and corn and
cook for 4 minutes.
Place in a bowl with
the capsicum, beans,
tomato, coriander and
lime juice. Marinate,
covered, for 30 minutes.
4. Lightly oil a chargrill
or heavy-based pan and
heat until it begins to
smoke. Brush the steaks
with oil and cook for
3–4 minutes on each
side for medium, or a
little longer for well-
done. Leave to stand
for 5 minutes before
serving with the salsa.

NUTRITION PER SERVE (6)
*Protein 20 g; Fat 3 g;
Carbohydrate 10 g; Dietary
Fibre 4 g; Cholesterol
45 mg; 635 kJ (150 cal)*

---

*Cheese and Bean Nachos (top) and
Beef with Black Bean Salsa*

Place the chillies under a preheated grill to blacken and blister their skins.

Place the chillies in a plastic bag to cool, then peel away the skin.

Chillies Rellenos (Stuffed Chillies)

Preparation time:
  30 minutes
Total cooking time:
  20 minutes
Serves 4 as a starter

8 green poblano chillies
1 cup (125 g/4 oz)
  grated Cheddar
plain flour, for dusting
3 eggs, separated
oil, for frying
1 cup (250 ml/8 fl oz)
  Red Chilli Sauce (see
  page 38)

1. Roast the chillies by placing under a preheated grill or holding carefully, one at a time, with tongs in an open gas flame, until the skin is black and blistered. Cool in a plastic bag, then carefully peel away the skin. Cut a slit in each chilli lengthways and remove the seeds and membrane, taking care not to break the chilli flesh.

2. Stuff the chillies with the cheese and press the slit closed, or secure with a toothpick. Dust with the flour and shake off the excess.

3. Whisk the egg whites until foamy, then add some salt and beat until stiff peaks form. Beat in the yolks, one at a time, until just combined.

4. Heat the oil about 2 cm (³/4 inch) deep in a frying pan. Dip the chillies into the egg, then fry, in batches, for 4–5 minutes, or until golden. Drain on paper towels and remove the toothpicks. Serve on a bed of red chilli sauce.

NUTRITION PER SERVE
Protein 20 g; Fat 15 g;
Carbohydrate 15 g; Dietary
Fibre 10 g; Cholesterol
165 mg; 1240 kJ (295 cal)

Chillies Rellenos

Slit the chillies lengthways, then remove the seeds and membrane.

Dust the stuffed chillies with the flour, then dip into the egg mixture.

Spicy Cowboy Beans

Preparation time:
  20 minutes + 1 hour standing
Total cooking time:
  1 hour 40 minutes
Serves 4–6

2¹/2 cups (525 g/
  1 lb 1 oz) dried red
  kidney beans
2 tablespoons oil
4 rashers bacon,
  chopped
1 large onion, chopped
2 teaspoons chilli
  powder
2 tablespoons
  Worcestershire sauce
¹/4 cup (55 g/1³/4 oz)
  firmly packed soft
  brown sugar
1 litre vegetable or beef
  stock

1. Place the beans in a large pan and cover with water. Bring to the boil, remove from the heat and let stand, covered, for 1 hour. Drain well.
2. Heat the oil in a large pan and add the bacon and onion. Cook, stirring occasionally, until the onion is golden and the bacon brown. Add the chilli powder and cook, stirring, for 30 seconds.
3. Add the beans, Worcestershire sauce, sugar and stock. Bring to the boil, reduce the heat to very low and cook, covered, for 1¹/2 hours, stirring occasionally and scraping the bottom of the pan. Serve with a little grated Cheddar sprinkled over.

NUTRITION PER SERVE (6)
Protein 8 g; Fat 8 g; Carbohydrate 20 g; Dietary Fibre 4 g; Cholesterol 10 mg; 730 kJ (170 cal)

Note: This dish tastes even better the next day. Thin with a little water if necessary when reheating.

Baked Honey and Garlic Ribs

Preparation time:
  20 minutes +
  overnight marinating
Total cooking time:
  55 minutes
Serves 4–6

1.5kg (2¹/2 lb)
  American-style pork
  ribs
¹/2 cup (175 g/5³/4 oz)
  honey
6 cloves garlic, crushed
5 cm (2 inch) piece
  ginger, finely grated
¹/4 teaspoon Tabasco 3
  tablespoons chilli
  sauce
2 teaspoons grated
  orange rind

1. Cut the ribs into small pieces, with about 2–3 bones per piece. Place in a large dish. Combine the remaining ingredients and pour over the ribs. Turn the ribs in the marinade until they are well coated. Leave in the refrigerator overnight to marinate if possible.
2. Preheat the oven to moderately hot 200°C (400°F/Gas 6). Drain the ribs and place the marinade in a small pan. Place the ribs in 1 or 2 large shallow ovenproof dishes in a single layer.
3. Bring the marinade to the boil and simmer gently for 3–4 minutes, or until it has thickened and reduced slightly.
4. Brush the ribs with the marinade and place in the oven. Cook for 50 minutes, basting with the marinade 3–4 times. Cook until the ribs are a rich golden colour and are well browned. Serve the ribs with jacket potatoes topped with a spoon of sour cream and a sprinkling of fresh chives.

NUTRITION PER SERVE (6)
Protein 35 g; Fat 70 g; Carbohydrate 25 g; Dietary Fibre 1 g; Cholesterol 250 mg; 3890 kJ (930 cal)

Spicy Cowboy Beans (top) and Baked Honey and Garlic Ribs

Black Bean and Roasted Garlic Dip

Preparation time:
  30 minutes + 1 hour standing
Total cooking time:
  2 hours 10 minutes
Serves 4

1/2 cup (110 g/3 3/4 oz) dried black beans
1 head garlic, cloves peeled and separated
2 tablespoons chopped fresh coriander
1/3 cup (80 ml/ 2 3/4 fl oz) lime juice
1/4 cup (60 g/2 oz) sour cream
pinch of chilli powder
dash of Tabasco sauce

1. Place the beans in a pan, cover with water and bring to the boil. Turn off the heat and leave to stand, covered, for 1 hour. Drain, refill with water, bring to the boil and simmer for 1 1/2 hours, until tender.
2. Meanwhile, preheat the oven to moderate 180°C (350°F/Gas 4). Place the garlic on a baking tray, drizzle over some oil and bake for 25–30 minutes, or until soft.
3. Place the beans in a large bowl and mash with a fork until they begin to break down and become slightly smooth. Mix in the garlic, coriander, lime juice, sour cream, chilli powder and Tabasco.
4. Serve with Corn Chips or some Cornbread (see page 23) sliced into 1 cm (1/2 inch) thick triangles and fried in a little oil until golden brown.

NUTRITION PER SERVE
Protein 3 g; Fat 4 g; Carbohydrate 3 g; Dietary Fibre 2 g; Cholesterol 13 mg; 260 kJ (60 cal)

Margarita Chicken with Black Bean Salsa

Preparation time:
  20 minutes + 1 hour standing + 2–4 hours marinating
Total cooking time:
  1 hour 15 minutes
Serves 6

6 chicken breast fillets
1/3 cup (80 ml/ 2 3/4 fl oz) tequila
1 cup (250 ml/8 fl oz) lime juice
1 cup (220 g/7 oz) dried black beans
1/3 cup (80 ml/ 2 3/4 fl oz) olive oil
1 teaspoon honey
1 clove garlic, crushed
440 g (14 oz) can corn kernels, drained
1 red onion, finely chopped
1/2 cup (15 g/1/2 oz) fresh coriander leaves, chopped

1. Place the chicken in a non-metallic dish and pour over the combined tequila and 2/3 cup (170 ml/5 1/2 fl oz) of the lime juice. Refrigerate, covered, for 2–4 hours, turning occasionally.
2. Place the beans in a pan, cover with water and bring to the boil. Turn off the heat and leave to stand, covered, for 1 hour. Drain, refill with water, bring to the boil and simmer for 1 hour, or until tender. Combine the remaining lime juice, oil, honey and garlic in a screw-top jar and shake until combined.
3. Drain the beans and allow to cool. Place in a bowl with the corn, onion and coriander. Pour the dressing over and toss to mix.
4. Heat a lightly oiled barbecue or chargrill pan. Remove the chicken from the marinade and cook for 4–5 minutes each side. Serve with the black bean salsa.

NUTRITION PER SERVE
Protein 45 g; Fat 15 g; Carbohydrate 25 g; Dietary Fibre 9 g; Cholesterol 80 mg; 1890 kJ (450 cal)

Black Bean and Roasted Garlic Dip (top) and Margarita Chicken with Black Bean Salsa

Tex-Mex Fried Chicken

Preparation time:
  15 minutes + 2 hours marinating
Total cooking time:
  30 minutes
Serves 4

1 kg (2 lb) chicken pieces, washed and dried
2 cups (500 ml/16 fl oz) buttermilk
oil, for deep-frying
1¹/2 cups(185 g/6 oz) plain flour

1. Place the chicken in a bowl and pour over the buttermilk. Mix well. Cover and refrigerate for 2 hours, turning occasionally.
2. Half fill a large, deep pan with oil and heat to 180°C (350°F). Place the flour in a shallow dish and season. Remove a piece of chicken from the buttermilk, shake off any excess, dip into the flour and coat well. Lower the chicken into the oil, in batches, and deep-fry for 12 minutes on each side, making sure that the oil is not too hot. Drain well on paper towels.

NUTRITION PER SERVE
Protein 70 g; Fat 30 g; Carbohydrate 40 g; Dietary Fibre 2 g; Cholesterol 135 mg; 2860 kJ (680 cal)

Charred Prawns with Capsicum Mayonnaise

Preparation time:
  20 minutes + 2 hours marinating
Total cooking time:
  40 minutes
Serves 4

1 kg (2 lb) large raw prawns
4 cloves garlic, crushed
3 tablespoons lime juice
1 teaspoon ground cumin
¹/2 cup (15 g/¹/2 oz) fresh coriander leaves, chopped
lime wedges, to serve

Capsicum Mayonnaise
1 small red capsicum
6 cloves garlic, unpeeled
1 tablespoon olive oil
¹/3 cup (90 g/3 oz) whole-egg mayonnaise
1 tablespoon lemon juice

1. Peel and devein the prawns, leaving the tails intact. Combine the garlic, lime juice, cumin and coriander in a bowl, place the prawns in the marinade and mix well. Cover and refrigerate for at least 2 hours.

2. To make the capsicum mayonnaise, preheat the oven to moderately hot 190ºC (375ºF/Gas 5). Cut the capsicum into quarters and remove the seeds and membrane. Place on a baking tray with the garlic and drizzle with the olive oil. Cook for 20–30 minutes, or until the skin blisters on the capsicum and the garlic is soft but not burnt. Place in a plastic bag until cool, then peel the skin off the capsicum and garlic.
3. Place in a food processor with the mayonnaise and process until fairly smooth. Place in a bowl and stir through the lemon juice.
4. Preheat a lightly oiled chargrill or heavy-based pan until it just starts to smoke. Drain the prawns, discarding the marinade and cook for 2 minutes on each side, or until cooked. You may need to do this in batches, depending on the size of your pan. Serve the prawns with the mayonnaise and a wedge of lime.

NUTRITION PER SERVE
Protein 50 g; Fat 15 g; Carbohydrate 8 g; Dietary Fibre 2 g; Cholesterol 380 mg; 1560 kJ (370 cal)

Tex-Mex Fried Chicken (top) and Charred Prawns with Capsicum Mayonnaise

Stuffed Sopaipillas

Preparation time:
  20 minutes
  + 20 minutes resting
Total cooking time:
  45 minutes
Serves 4

Sopaipillas
4 cups (500 g/1 lb)
  plain flour
1¹/2 teaspoons baking
  powder
20 g (³/4 oz) butter
1¹/2 cups (375 ml/12 fl
  oz) boiled milk,
  cooled
oil, for deep-frying
1 cup (250 ml/8 fl oz)
  Red Chilli Sauce (see
  page 38)
1¹/2 cups (185 g/6 oz)
  grated Cheddar

Filling
2 tablespoons oil
450 g (14¹/4 oz) pork
  mince
1 red onion, chopped
¹/4 teaspoon cayenne
  pepper

1 clove garlic, crushed
100 ml (3¹/4 fl oz)
  chicken stock
180 g (5³/4 oz) Refried
  Beans (ready-made or
  see page 63)
2 tablespoons chopped
  fresh coriander

1. To make the
sopaipillas, combine the
flour, baking powder
and 1¹/2 teaspoons salt
in a bowl. Rub in the
butter and mix until it
resembles breadcrumbs.
Gradually work in the
milk until the dough is
stiff and springy. Knead
15–20 times, or until
smooth, then rest,
covered, for 20 minutes.
2. To make the filling,
heat the oil and add the
pork mince, onion,
pepper and garlic;
season, then cook for
10 minutes. Add the
stock, simmer for 10
minutes, then add the
beans and coriander.
3. Preheat the oven to

moderate 180°C
(350°F/Gas 4). Divide
the dough into 8 pieces
and place on an
unfloured surface.
Roll each piece into a
5 mm (¹/4 inch) thick,
10 cm (4 inch) square.
Keep covered.
4. In a pan, heat 6 cm
(2¹/2 inches) of oil to
about 180°C (350°F).
Lightly stretch each
square, then place in
the oil. Hold under for
20 seconds each side, or
until puffed and golden.
Drain on paper towels.
5. Slit each sopaipilla
open at one end and
spoon in the filling.
Place in an ovenproof
dish and spoon over
some of the chilli sauce
and Cheddar. Bake for
15 minutes, then serve
with extra chilli sauce.

NUTRITION PER SERVE
*Protein 35 g; Fat 45 g;
Carbohydrate 100 g; Dietary
Fibre 9 g; Cholesterol
80 mg; 3900 kJ (930 cal)*

Stuffed Sopaipillas

*Pour in the milk and mix with a flat-
bladed knife until the dough is stiff.*

*Knead the dough on a lightly floured
surface until it is smooth.*

With tongs, hold a square of the dough under the hot oil until puffed and golden.

Slit each sopaipilla at one end and spoon in the filling.

Spicy Mexican Meatball Soup

Preparation time:
  20 minutes
Total cooking time:
  30 minutes
Serves 4

250 g (8 oz) minced
  beef
250 g (8 oz) minced
  pork
3/4 cup (140 g/4 1/2 oz)
  cooked white rice
1 egg, lightly beaten
1/2 teaspoon chilli
  powder
1/2 teaspoon paprika
1 teaspoon salt
2 tablespoons olive oil
1 small onion, diced
1 clove garlic, crushed
1 1/4 cups (315 ml/
  10 fl oz) tomato purée
1 litre beef stock
1/4 cup (15 g/1/2 oz)
  finely chopped fresh
  oregano

1. Combine the beef,
pork, rice, egg, chilli
powder, paprika and
salt in a bowl. Shape
into balls the size of
walnuts and set aside.
2. Heat the oil in a
saucepan and gently fry
the onion and garlic
over medium-low heat
until soft. Stir in the
tomato purée and beef
stock. Bring to the boil
and drop in the
meatballs. Cover and
simmer for about
20 minutes.
3. Serve with some
chopped oregano
sprinkled over.

NUTRITION PER SERVE
*Protein 20 g; Fat 30 g;
Carbohydrate 12 g; Dietary
Fibre 2 g; Cholesterol
90 mg; 1815 kJ (430 cal)*

Corn and Coriander Soup

Preparation time:
  20 minutes
Total cooking time:
  50 minutes
Serves 4–6

8 corn cobs
1 large red capsicum
2 tablespoons oil
1 onion, finely chopped
2 cloves garlic, crushed
3 cups (750 ml/24 fl oz)
  chicken stock
1/2 cup (125 ml/4 fl oz)
  lime juice
1/3 cup (10 g/1/4 oz)
  fresh coriander leaves

1. Preheat a barbecue
or grill. Remove the
husks and silk from the
corn cobs and cook on
the barbecue or grill for
about 10 minutes,
turning frequently, until
roasted and slightly
blackened. Cool, then
cut the kernels from the
cobs with a small,
sharp knife. (Hold the
cobs vertically on a
chopping board and
run the knife down the
sides of the cobs.)
2. Cut the capsicum
into quarters. Discard
the seeds and
membrane and cook
under the grill or on the
barbecue until the skin
has blackened and
blistered. Remove from
the heat and place in a
plastic bag to cool. Peel
away the skin and
finely chop the flesh.
3. Heat the oil in a
large pan, and cook the
onion for 5 minutes, or
until very soft and
lightly golden. Add the
garlic and cook for
1 minute.
4. Add the corn
kernels, capsicum and
chicken stock to the
pan, bring to the boil,
reduce the heat and
simmer, partially
covered, for about
20 minutes.
5. Cool the soup
slightly, then purée
half of it in a blender or
food processor until
the mixture is fairly
smooth. Transfer all the
soup to a clean pan to
heat through (do not
boil). Just before
serving, stir through the
lime juice and the
coriander leaves.

NUTRITION PER SERVE (6)
*Protein 8 g; Fat 9 g;
Carbohydrate 50 g; Dietary
Fibre 8 g; Cholesterol
0 mg; 1300 kJ (310 cal)*

*Spicy Mexican Meatball Soup (top) with
Corn and Coriander Soup*

Fried Onion Rings

Preparation time:
  10 minutes
Total cooking time:
  20 minutes
Serves 4–6 as a snack

2 large onions
1¹/2 cups (185 g/6 oz)
  plain flour
2 teaspoons ground
  cumin
1 teaspoon paprika
1¹/2 cups (375ml/
  12 fl oz) cold beer
oil, for deep-frying
Red Chilli Sauce (see
  page 38) or sweet
  chilli sauce, to serve

1. Cut the onions into rings about 1 cm (¹/2 inch) wide. Sift the flour and spices together into a large bowl, make a well in the centre and slowly pour in the beer. Stir in lightly with a fork until just combined, taking care not to overbeat or the batter will not be light and crisp. The mixture should be slightly lumpy.
2. Half-fill a large pan with the oil. Heat until moderately hot (when a bread cube dropped in becomes crisp and golden in 45 seconds, the oil is ready). Dip the onion rings into the batter, allowing the excess to drip off, then deep-fry in batches until crisp and golden. Drain well on paper towels. Season with salt, then serve with the red chilli or sweet chilli sauce on the side.

NUTRITION PER SERVE (6)
Protein 5 g; Fat 15 g; Carbohydrate 40 g; Dietary Fibre 0 g; Cholesterol 30 mg; 1295 kJ (310 cal)

Chilli Chicken Chimichangas

Preparation time:
  40 minutes
Total cooking time:
  30 minutes
Serves 6

4 chicken breast fillets
2 teaspoons pepper
1 teaspoon chilli
  powder
¹/2 cup (125 ml/4 fl oz)
  oil
2 cloves garlic
¹/2 teaspoon chilli
  powder, extra
500 g (1 lb) button
  mushrooms, sliced
6 flour tortillas (ready-
  made or see page 22)
Fresh Tomato Salsa (see
  page 9)

1. Preheat the oven to warm 160°C (315°F/ Gas 2–3). Sprinkle the chicken with the pepper and chilli powder. Heat half the oil in a frying pan, add the chicken and cook for about 3–4 minutes on each side, or until cooked through. Cool, then shred into fine pieces, using 2 forks to pull the meat apart. Add the remaining oil to the pan and lightly fry the garlic and extra chilli powder for 1 minute. Add the mushrooms and stir-fry for about 3–4 minutes. Add the chicken and toss to combine. Set aside.
2. Wrap the tortillas in foil and place in the oven for 10 minutes to soften. Work quickly with one tortilla at a time, keeping the others covered with the foil. Place some filling in the centre and top with 2 tablespoons of the tomato salsa. Fold in the sides and roll up like an envelope.
3. Heat a little oil in a frying pan. Place 1–2 filled tortillas in the hot oil at once, turning carefully to cook both sides until they are lightly golden. Serve with the remaining tomato salsa, some Mexican Rice (page 63) and a spoonful of sour cream.

NUTRITION PER SERVE
Protein 6.5 g; Fat 30 g; Carbohydrate 25 g; Dietary Fibre 5 g; Cholesterol 50 mg; 2025 kJ (340 cal)

Fried Onion Rings (top) with Chilli Chicken Chimichangas

Rub the butter into the flour mixture until it resembles breadcrumbs.

Pour in the beef stock and stir into the mixture with a flat-bladed knife.

Tamale Beef and Bean Pie

Preparation time:
  40 minutes
Total cooking time:
  1 hour 30 minutes
Serves 6–8

1 tablespoon oil
1 large onion, finely
  chopped
500 g (1 lb) beef mince
3 cloves garlic, crushed
1/2 teaspoon chilli
  powder
400 g (12³/4 oz) can
  crushed tomatoes
1 cup (250 ml/8 fl oz)
  beef stock
425 g (13¹/2 oz) can
  red kidney beans,
  drained
2¹/2 cups (360 g/
  11¹/2 oz) masa harina
1 teaspoon baking
  powder
125 g (4 oz) butter,
  cut into cubes and
  chilled
1¹/2 cups (375 ml/
  12 fl oz) beef stock
2 cups (250 g/8 oz)
  grated Cheddar

1. Heat the oil in a frying pan. Add the onion and cook gently until soft and transparent. Increase the heat, add the mince and cook until brown. Add the garlic, chilli, tomatoes and stock. Bring to the boil, then simmer for 30 minutes, or until the liquid has evaporated to a thick sauce. Stir in the beans and cool.
2. Lightly grease a deep 23 cm (9 inch) pie dish. Place the masa harina, baking powder and 1/2 teaspoon salt in a bowl. Rub in the butter until the mixture resembles breadcrumbs. Using a knife, mix in the stock, then use your hands to bring the mixture together into a ball. Divide in half and roll one half between 2 sheets of baking paper to fit the dish.
3. Push the pastry into the dish and up the side, not worrying if the pastry cracks. Trim the edge.
4. Preheat the oven to moderately hot 200°C (400°F/Gas 6). Place the filling into the dish and sprinkle with half the Cheddar. Roll out the remaining pastry in the same way as before. Brush the edge with water and place on top. Trim the edge and press the 2 layers of pastry together to seal. Sprinkle with the remaining Cheddar and bake for 45 minutes, or until the pastry is crisp and slightly puffed. Decorate with a little sour cream to serve.

NUTRITION PER SERVE (8)
Protein 25 g; Fat 30 g; Carbohydrate 10 g; Dietary Fibre 5 g; Cholesterol 110 mg; 1820 kJ (435 cal)

Tamale Beef and Bean Pie

Divide the dough in half and roll out 1 half between 2 sheets of baking paper.

Spoon the beef and bean filling into the dish, then sprinkle with cheese.

Guacamole

Preparation time:
  30 minutes
Total cooking time:
  Nil
Serves 6 as a side dish

3 avocados
1 small tomato
1–2 red chillies, finely
  chopped
1 small red onion,
  finely chopped
1 tablespoon chopped
  fresh coriander
1 tablespoon lime juice
2 tablespoons sour
  cream
1–2 drops habanero or
  Tabasco sauce

1. Cut the avocados in
half, discarding the skin
and stone. Roughly
chop, then mash lightly
with a fork.
2. Cut the tomato in
half horizontally. Using
a teaspoon, scoop out
the seeds and discard.
Finely dice the flesh and
add to the avocado.
3. Stir in the chilli,
onion, coriander, lime
juice, sour cream and
habanero or Tabasco
sauce. Season with
cracked black pepper.
4. Serve immediately, or
cover wih plastic wrap
and refrigerate for up
to 2 hours, removing
30 minutes before
serving to allow the
guacamole to reach
room temperature.

NUTRITION PER SERVE
*Protein 1 g; Fat 8 g;
Carbohydrate 1 g; Dietary
Fibre 0 g; Cholesterol
2 mg; 300 kJ (70 cal)*

Note: Habanero sauce
is a very hot sauce
made from habanero
chillies. Use sparingly
to add extra zing.

Beef Tacos

Preparation time:
  30 minutes
Total cooking time:
  20 minutes
Serves 4

1 tablespoon oil
1 onion, finely chopped
2 cloves garlic, finely
  chopped
1/4 teaspoon chilli
  powder
1 teaspoon ground
  paprika
1 teaspoon ground
  cumin
1 teaspoon ground
  coriander
1/2 teaspoon dried
  oregano
1 teaspoon sugar
500 g (1 lb) lean beef
  mince
2 tablespoons tomato
  paste
12 small taco shells
4 large lettuce leaves,
  shredded
1 1/2 cups (185 g/6 oz)
  grated Cheddar
Fresh Tomato Salsa (see
  page 9), to serve

1. Preheat the oven to
moderate 180°C
(350°F/Gas 4). Heat the
oil in a large frying
pan. Add the onion and
cook over low heat
until softened but not
browned. Add the
garlic and cook for a
further minute. Stir in
the chilli powder,
paprika, cumin,
coriander, oregano, the
sugar and a teaspoon
of salt. Cook over
medium heat for
3–4 minutes.
2. Increase the heat,
add the beef mince and
cook until the meat is
browned. Add about
3 tablespoons water,
making sure that the
pan is hot so that most
of the water
evaporates. Stir the
mixture constantly for
5–10 minutes. If the
beef sticks, add a little
more water. The
mixture will be quite
dry looking, but will
have plenty of flavour.
3. Heat the taco
shells in the oven for
5 minutes. Place the
meat on the table with
the taco shells, lettuce,
Cheddar and tomato
salsa and let everyone
assemble the tacos
themselves.

NUTRITION PER SERVE
*Protein 40 g; Fat 40 g;
Carbohydrate 4 g; Dietary
Fibre 2 g; Cholesterol
125 mg; 2200 kJ (525 cal)*

Guacamole (top) and Beef Tacos

Creamed Corn

Preparation time:
  15 minutes
Total cooking time:
  5 minutes
Serves 8 as a side dish

420 g (13¹/4 oz) can
  corn kernels
4 teaspoons cornflour

1. Drain the corn
kernels, reserving the
liquid. Add a little
water to the liquid if
necessary to make up
³/4 cup (185 ml/6 fl oz).
Place 200 g (6¹/2 oz) of
the corn kernels in a
food processor with the
reserved liquid and
process until smooth.
2. Transfer to a heavy-
based saucepan. In a
bowl, mix the cornflour
with a little water to
form a smooth paste.
3. Add the cornflour
paste to the pan with
the remaining corn
kernels and stir over
medium heat until the
mixture thickens and
boils. Set aside to cool
slightly as the mixture
will thicken on
standing. Serve as a
side dish.

NUTRITION PER SERVE
Protein 0 g; Fat 0 g;
Carbohydrate 3 g; Dietary
Fibre 0 g; Cholesterol
0 mg; 66 kJ (16 cal)

Mexican Rice

Preparation time:
  10 minutes
Total cooking time:
  25 minutes
Serves 8 as a side dish

1 tablespoon olive oil
1 small onion, chopped
1 clove garlic, chopped
1 cup (200 g/6¹/2 oz)
  long-grain white rice
¹/2 cup (125 ml/4 fl oz)
  tomato purée
1 cup (250 ml/8 fl oz)
  chicken stock

1. Heat the oil in a
large pan, add the
onion and cook for
5 minutes, or until soft.
Add the garlic and
cook for 1 minute. Add
the rice and stir for
1–2 minutes, or until
well coated in the oil.
2. Add the tomato
purée and stock to the
pan and bring to the
boil. Reduce the heat to
very low, cover tightly
with a lid and simmer
for 25 minutes, or until
the liquid is absorbed
and the rice tender.
Fluff up the grains with
a fork, and serve as a
side dish.

NUTRITION PER SERVE
Protein 2 g; Fat 3 g;
Carbohydrate 20 g; Dietary
Fibre 1 g; Cholesterol
0 mg; 490 kJ (115 cal)

Refried Beans

Preparation time:
  10 minutes +
  overnight soaking
Total cooking time:
  1 hour 45 minutes
Serves 8 as a side dish

1 cup (200 g/6¹/2 oz)
  dried pinto, red
  kidney or black beans
1 small onion, halved
3 cloves garlic
3 tablespoons oil

1. Place the beans in a
bowl, cover with water
and soak overnight.
Drain. Place in a heavy-
based pan and cover
with water.
2. Add the onion and
garlic, bring to the boil,
reduce the heat and
simmer for 1¹/2 hours,
or until tender. Cool,
then remove the onion
and garlic. Drain the
beans, reserving
¹/2 cup (125 ml/4 fl oz)
of the liquid.
3. Heat the oil in a
heavy-based frying pan.
Add half the beans and
mash. Stir in half the
liquid, then add the
remaining beans and
liquid and mash to a
thick purée. Serve at
once, or refrigerate for
up to 2 days.

NUTRITION PER SERVE
Protein 4 g; Fat 7 g;
Carbohydrate 4 g; Dietary
Fibre 3 g; Cholesterol
0 mg; 400 kJ (95 cal)

Creamed Corn (top), Mexican Rice, and
Refried Beans (bottom)

Index